Bats

Megan Cullis

Designed by Helen Edmonds and Sam Chandler

Illustrated by Connie McLennan and Sue King

Bat consultant: Dr. Anthony Wardhaugh

Reading consultant: Alison Kelly, Roehampton University

Contents

A world of bats

Bats are flying animals that come out at night. Over a thousand different types of bats live around the world.

Bats often set off to hunt in big groups.

The smallest bat is the same size as a bumblebee.

On the wing

Bats are furry animals that fly. Their wings are made of thin, stretchy skin.

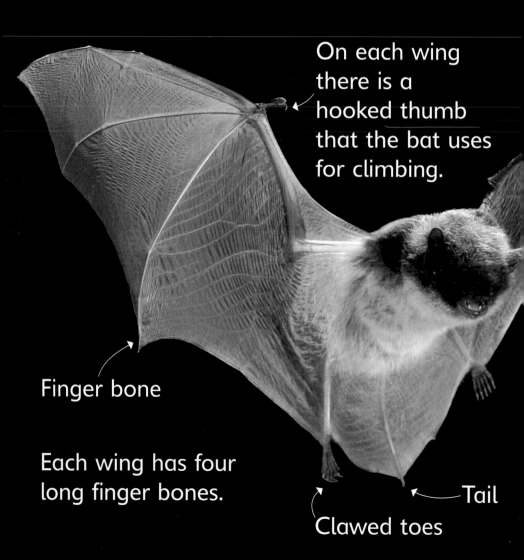

On each wing there is a hooked thumb that the bat uses for climbing.

Finger bone

Each wing has four long finger bones.

Clawed toes

Tail

Bat wings tear easily but the skin heals quickly.

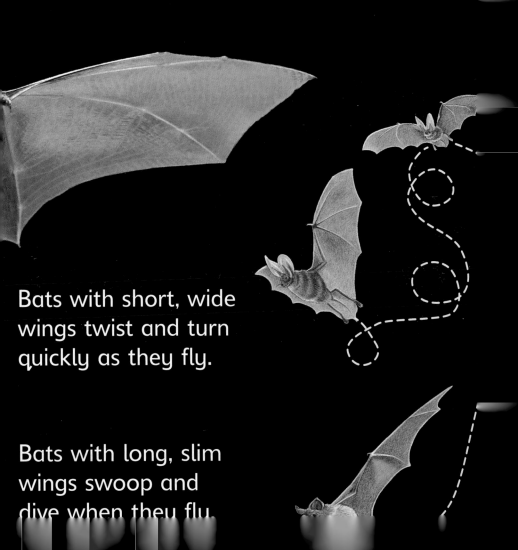

Bats with short, wide wings twist and turn quickly as they fly.

Bats with long, slim wings swoop and dive when they fly.

Sleeping tight

Bats are nocturnal. This means they stay awake at night and sleep during the day.

Bats that live in hot places sleep outside to keep cool. They rest in groups to feel safe from enemies, such as snakes and birds.

Some bats sleep inside caves to shelter from the wind and rain.

A horseshoe bat finds a cave where it can sleep.

It hangs upside down from the cave roof with its toes.

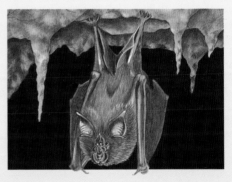

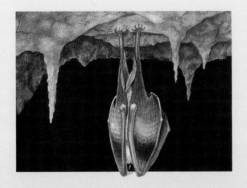

It wraps its wings around its body and head to keep dry.

Fur coats

All bats have furry bodies, but they have different types of fur.

Hoary bats have thick, fluffy fur that keeps them warm when it is very cold.

 Bats comb their fur with their claws to keep it clean.

Ghost bats have smooth, silver fur and pale skin.

Spotted bats have black and white patches on their fur.

White-lined bats have two thin wiggly lines along their backs.

Sensing sounds

Many bats find their way in the dark using their ears instead of their eyes.

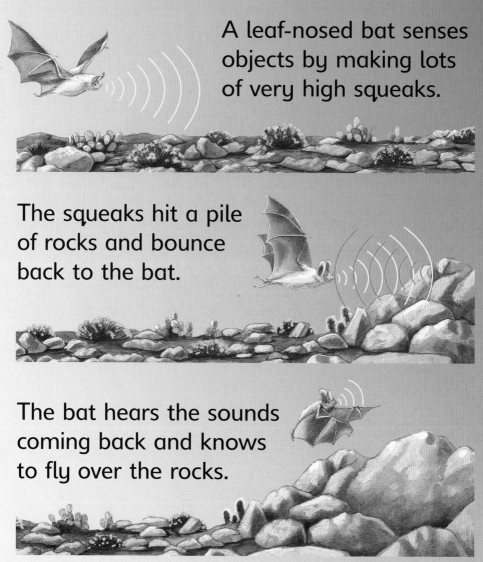

A leaf-nosed bat senses objects by making lots of very high squeaks.

The squeaks hit a pile of rocks and bounce back to the bat.

The bat hears the sounds coming back and knows to fly over the rocks.

Bats also use squeaks to hunt for insects in the dark.

Some bats squeak up to 200 times a second.

Secret lives

Some bats have clever ways of hiding among trees, so hungry enemies can't see them.

Sharp-nosed bats rest on tree trunks. Their speckled fur is hard to see against the bark.

Golden-tipped bats hide in bird nests. Their fur looks like moss.

These tiny tent-making bats have made a shelter from a big leaf.

They do this by biting along the middle of a leaf so the sides drop down.

The leaf makes a tent shape and a group of bats hangs inside it.

Baby bats

A baby bat is called a pup. Mother bats often gather together to raise their pups.

1. A pipistrelle pup is born blind and without much fur.

2. It crawls over to other newborn pups to keep warm.

3. A few days later its eyes open and its fur starts to grow.

4. At three weeks old, the pup is ready to fly on its own.

Fruit bat pups
stay very close to their
mothers until they can fly.

Insect eaters

Lots of bats eat insects.

This horseshoe bat is flying through the air hunting for moths.

Pallid bats fly along the ground searching for grasshoppers.

Some leaf-nosed bats perch on trees waiting for insects to fly by.

The bat grabs a moth
between its wings and
flicks it into its mouth.

Bechstein's bats pick
beetles from the
leaves of trees.

Some short-tailed
bats hunt for crickets
on forest floors.

17

Sweet treats

Bats that live in hot places often eat fruit and drink sweet juices from flowers.

A long-tongued bat searches for flowers that open at night.

It smells some flowers and hovers close by.

The bat sticks out its long tongue and drinks the juice.

Fruit bats find fruit using their big, beady eyes and good sense of smell.

The tube-lipped nectar bat has a tongue that is longer than its body.

Splashing around

Many bats fly over ponds
and lakes to drink the water.
Other bats hunt for fish.

This long-eared myotis is drinking
big gulps of water as it flies along.

A Daubenton's bat
skims over the water
searching for food.

It senses some
ripples and splashes
made by a fish.

The bat stretches out its big feet into the water.

It grabs the fish and quickly scoops it into its mouth.

Funny faces

Some bats have very strange faces.

Brown long-eared bats have huge ears that pick up very quiet sounds.

Spear-nosed bats have pointed noses to make their squeaks sound clearer.

Wrinkle-faced bats have crinkly skin all over their faces. No one is sure why.

This hammer-headed bat has big lips and a frilly snout. It uses them to make loud honking sounds.

Ghost-faced bats look as if their eyes are inside their ears.

A vampire bite

Vampire bats drink blood. They feed on the blood of birds, farm animals and sometimes even people.

This vampire bat is showing its sharp front teeth. It uses them to bite through skin.

1. A vampire bat finds a sleeping cow.

2. It jumps quietly onto the cow's body.

3. It bites a tiny cut on the cow's neck...

4. ...and softly licks up the blood.

Vampire bats can turn cartwheels in the air.

Coping with the cold

During cold winters, food is hard to find, so some bats fall into a long, deep sleep. This is called hibernating.

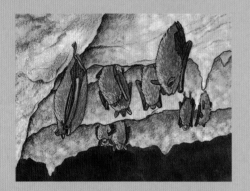

Little brown bats sleep together inside cool, damp caves.

Barbastelle bats crawl inside hollow tree trunks to sleep.

Pipistrelle bats sleep inside the walls of old stone buildings.

In spring it gets warmer and hibernating bats wake up.

This noctule bat is leaving its winter tree hole to hunt for food.

Some bats fly to warmer places to escape cold winters.

Bats in danger

In many countries, bats are dying out because people do things that harm them.

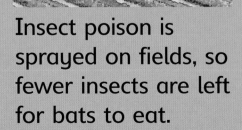

People cut down trees and forests for wood, destroying bats' homes.

Insect poison is sprayed on fields, so fewer insects are left for bats to eat.

Many people are helping to protect bats. Over a million bats live safely under a bridge in Austin, Texas, U.S.A.

People attach bat boxes to tree trunks to make safe homes for bats.

Gates are built on caves to stop people from disturbing any bats inside.

Glossary

Here are some of the words in this book you might not know. This page tells you what they mean.

 swoop - to fly down quickly and smoothly through the air.

 nocturnal - awake and busy at night. Nocturnal animals rest during the day.

 pup - a baby bat. Mother bats usually have one pup each year.

 hunt - to look for, catch and kill animals, usually to eat.

 hover - to stay in one place in the air. Bats flap their wings very quickly.

 snout - the long nose and mouth parts of an animal's face.

 hibernation - a long, deep sleep that usually lasts all winter.

Websites to visit

You can visit exciting websites to find out more about bats.

To visit these websites, go to the Usborne Quicklinks Website at **www.usborne-quicklinks.com** Read the internet safety guidelines, and then type the keywords "**beginners bats**".

The websites are regularly reviewed and the links in Usborne Quicklinks are updated. However, Usborne Publishing is not responsible, and does not accept liability, for the content or availability of any website other than its own. We recommend that children are supervised while on the internet.

Grey long-eared bats listen for the sounds of fluttering moths.

Index

Acknowledgements

Photographic manipulation by John Russell

Photo credits
The publishers are grateful to the following for permission to reproduce material:
© **Biosphoto/Dziubak Franck & Christine** 13; © **Biosphoto/Mafart-Renodier Alain** 1;
© **Digital Visions** cover background; © **Frank Harrison** 6; © **Fred Bruemmer/Still Pictures** 2-3;
© **Fritz Polking/FLPA** 28-29; © **Hugh Clark/FLPA** 31;
© **Hugh Maynard/naturepl.com** 23; © **Ingo Schulz/Photolibrary.com** 12;
© **Michael Durham/Minden Pictures/FLPA** 8; © **Michael Durham/Minden Pictures/National Geographic Stock** 4-5; © **Michael & Patricia Fogden/Minden Pictures/FLPA** 24;
© **Mike Read/naturepl.com** 27; © **Minden Pictures/Michael Durham** 11, 20-21; © **NHPA/Stephen Dalton** 16-17; © **PetStockBoys/Alamy** 19; © **Silvestris Fotoservice/FLPA** cover photograph;
© **Win-Initiative/Getty Images** 15.

Every effort has been made to trace and acknowledge ownership of copyright. If any rights have been omitted, the publishers offer to rectify this in any subsequent editions following notification.